D0852613

WORLD OF INSECTS

Dragonflies

by Emily K. Green

BELLWETHER MEDIA • MINNEAPOLIS, MN

BLASTOFF!
2
READERS

Note to Librarians, Teachers, and Parents:

Blastoff! Readers are carefully developed by literacy experts and combine standards-based content with developmentally appropriate text.

Level 1 provides the most support through repetition of high-frequency words, light text, predictable sentence patterns, and strong visual support.

Level 2 offers early readers a bit more challenge through varied simple sentences, increased text load, and less repetition of high-frequency words.

Level 3 advances early-fluent readers toward fluency through increased text and concept load, less reliance on visuals, longer sentences, and more literary language.

Whichever book is right for your reader, Blastoff! Readers are the perfect books to build confidence and encourage a love of reading that will last a lifetime!

This edition first published in 2007 by Bellwether Media.

No part of this publication may be reproduced in whole or in part without written permission of the publisher. For information regarding permission, write to Bellwether Media Inc., Attention: Permissions Department, Post Office Box 1C, Minnetonka, MN 55345-9998.

Library of Congress Cataloging-in-Publication Data
Green, Emily K., 1966-
 Dragonflies / by Emily K. Green.
  p. cm. — (Blastoff! readers) (World of insects)
Summary: "Simple text accompanied by full-color photographs give an up-close look at dragonflies."
 Includes bibliographical references and index.
 ISBN-10: 1-60014-012-2 (hardcover : alk. paper) 37579579   5/08
 ISBN-13: 978-1-60014-012-9 (hardcover : alk. paper)
 1. Dragonflies—Juvenile literature. I. Title. II. Series.

QL520.G735 2006
595.7'33—dc22   2006005335

Text copyright © 2007 by Bellwether Media.
Printed in the United States of America.

Table of Contents

Dragonflies are **insects**.
But they are not **flies**.

Dragonflies live near streams, lakes, and ponds.

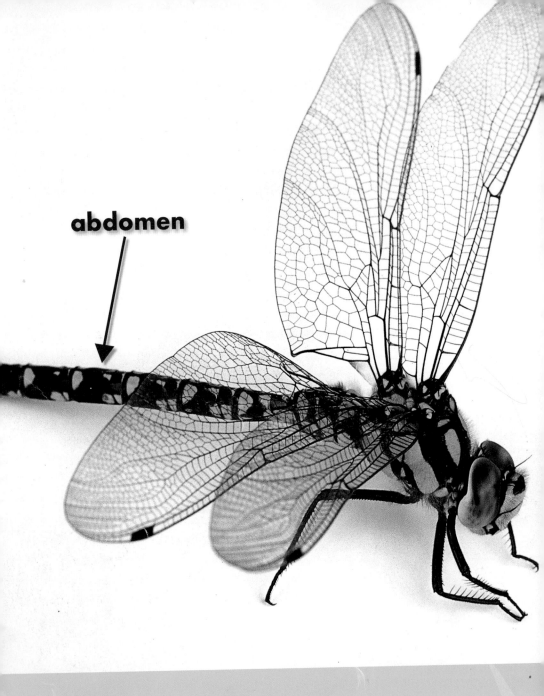

abdomen

A dragonfly has a long, skinny **abdomen**.

Dragonflies can be blue, green, yellow, red, and other colors. Some look spotted.

eyes

A dragonfly has two
big eyes.

They can see all around
without moving their heads.

A dragonfly has six legs.

But most dragonflies do not walk. They stand and rest on their legs.

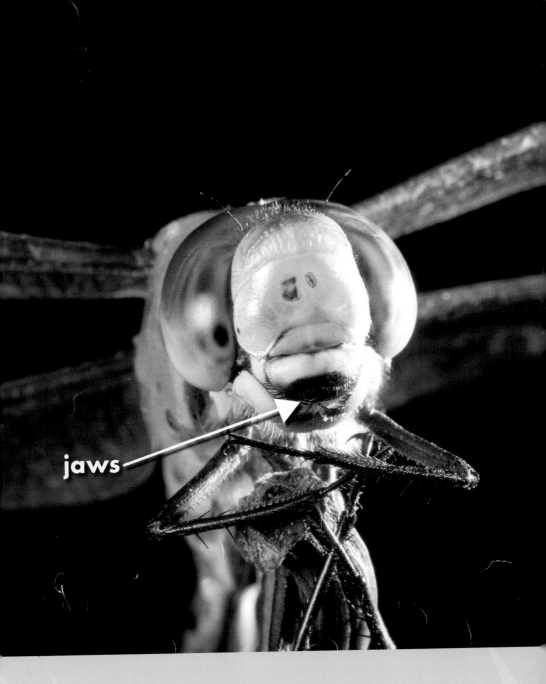

jaws

A dragonfly has big,
strong **jaws**.

They use their jaws to catch
and eat small insects.
Dragonflies do not bite people.

A dragonfly has four
strong wings.

14

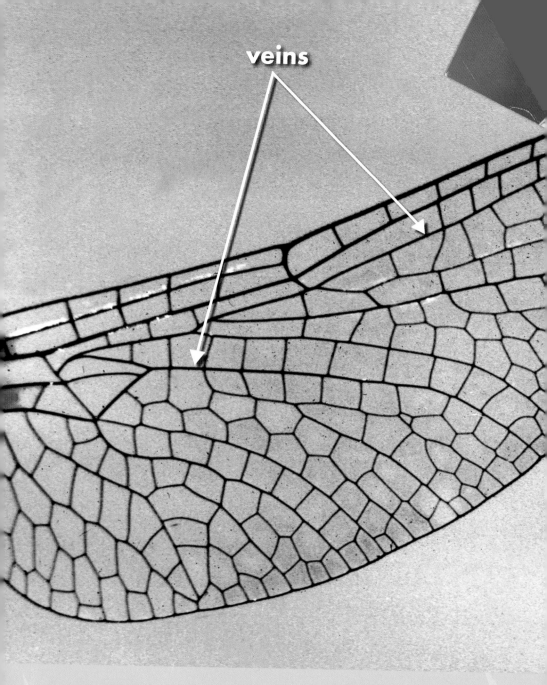

veins

Tiny lines called **veins** cover
their wings.

Dragonflies rest with their
wings spread out.

Dragonflies can fly as
fast as some birds.

Dragonflies can **hover** in place like a helicopter.

18

They can even fly backward.
Then dragonflies must rest.

This dragonfly stops to eat an insect it caught.

Some people say dragonflies bring good luck. What do you think?

Glossary

abdomen—the long skinny end of a dragonfly's body

flies—a kind of insect; most flies have only two wings; some flies have no wings.

hover—to stay in one place in the air

insect—a kind of animal that has a hard body; most insects also have two antennas, six legs, and two or four wings.

jaws—the bottom part of the dragonfly's mouth; a dragonfly chews food with its jaws.

veins—tiny tubes that run across the dragonflies' wings

To Learn More

AT THE LIBRARY

Allen, Judy and Tudor Humphries. *Are You a Dragonfly?* New York: Kingfisher, 2001.

Lively, Penelope. *One, Two, Three, Jump!* New York: Margaret K. McElderry Books, 1999.

Morris, Ting. *Dragonfly.* Mankato, Minn.: Smart Apple Media, 2005.

Rinehart, Susie Caldwell. *Eliza and the Dragonfly.* Nevada City, Calif.: Dawn Publications, 2004.

ON THE WEB
Learning more about dragonflies is as easy as 1, 2, 3.

1. Go to www.factsurfer.com

2. Enter "dragonflies" into search box.

3. Click the "Surf" button and you will see a list of related web sites.

With factsurfer.com, finding more information is just a click away.

Index